REAL STINKERS

600 JOKES TO MAKE YOU GO EWWW!

 KIM T. GRISWELL

STERLING CHILDREN'S BOOKS
New York

To Jeff, Joe, Sean, Nick, Will, Steven, and Rob.
I couldn't do this without EWWW!

STERLING CHILDREN'S BOOKS
New York

An Imprint of Sterling Publishing Co., Inc.
1166 Avenue of the Americas
New York, NY 10036

ISBN 978-1-4549-3215-4

Distributed in Canada by Sterling Publishing Co., Inc.
C/o Canadian Manda Group, 664 Annette Street
Toronto, Ontario M6S 2C8, Canada
Distributed in the United Kingdom by GMC Distribution Services
Castle Place, 166 High Street, Lewes, East Sussex BN7 1XU, England
Distributed in Australia by NewSouth Books
University of New South Wales, Sydney, NSW 2052, Australia

For information about custom editions, special sales, and premium
and corporate purchases, please contact Sterling Special Sales
at 800-805-5489 or specialsales@sterlingpublishing.com.

Manufactured in Canada

Lot #:
2 4 6 8 10 9 7 5 3 1
04/02

sterlingpublishing.com

Cover illustration by Julie Robine
Cover and interior art components by iStock and Shutterstock
Cover and interior design by Julie Robine

HA HA HA HA
HA HA HA HA
HA

Contents

BEGINNER'S YUCK

If a kid ate her parents, what would that make her?
An orphan.

- -

What's more disgusting, a pail of puke or a store-owner's son?
A store-owner's son. He's always a little grocer.

- -

Why did the kid stuff his dad in the freezer?
He wanted a cold pop.

- -

Why did the tuba player eat a bean burrito?
He wanted louder toots.

- -

What did the blind skunk do?
He fell in love with a fart.

WOOPS

- -

GRODYNITION
Eyedropper: a clumsy eye doctor.

- -

Why did Captain Hook get a nosebleed?
He picked his nose with the wrong hand.

GRODY GREG: Why did you tell everyone I'm disgusting?

GRIMEY GERT: I didn't know you were keeping it a secret.

What kind of brush should you never use on your hair?

A toothbrush.

FOUL FACT

A pumping heart can shoot blood more than 30 feet!

What has six legs and constantly drools?

Teething triplets.

How do monsters like their eggs?

Terror-fried.

How did the blind carpenter regain his sight?

He picked up a hammer and saw.

HAHA

What do you get when you cross an elephant with a goldfish?

You get to clean the fishbowl every day.

What was the kitten's favorite fable?

The Tortoise and the Hairball.

FOUL FACT

A pill bug can drink through its butt.

What do you get when you cross a serial killer with a pair of jeans?

Jack the Zipper.

GRODYNITION

Cannibal Graduation Card: Congratulations on the grads-u-ate!

When should you sleep in a salad?

When you need to wake up oilier.

What do you get when you cross a mosquito with a lollipop?

A bloodsucker.

HA HA HA HA HA HA
HA HA HA HA HA HA HA HA

When does a woman have to shave twenty times a day?

When she's a barber.

Which bug can tell time?

A clock-roach.

LUNCH LADY: Hey, kid! Why'd you pick the raisins out of your oatmeal cookie?

KID: I didn't. They crawled out by themselves.

Why do giants stomp on people?

They like the squishy feeling between their toes.

What was the name of the Big Bad Wolf's favorite pig?

Chris P. Bacon.

How are Frankenstein's toes attached to his feet?

With toe nails.

What happened when the skunk fell into the river?

It stank to the bottom.

FOUL FACT

Belgium has an underwear museum. For undies to be exhibited, they must have been worn at least once by a famous person.

What's worse than an elephant with bad breath?

A millipede with stinky feet.

How are grandma's teeth like stars?

They come out a night.

EWWW

GRODYNITION

Ringleader: first one in the bathtub.

GHOUL: I'm glad you could come to dinner.

GHOULFRIEND: Your mom made a tasty meal.

Why are chicken coops so disgusting?

They're full of fowl things.

What kind of manure do you find in a henhouse?

Cock-a-doodle poo!

Why did the maid quit her job?

Grime doesn't pay.

HA HA HA HA HA HA

What color is a hiccup?

Burple.

Which surgeon kills all of his patients?

Dr. E. Vile.

FOUL FACT

Two pugnose eels were found living inside a mako shark's heart.

What is a vampire's favorite kind of road.

A main artery.

BAND MEMBER: Help! I swallowed my flute.

SCHOOL NURSE: Be glad you don't play the tuba!

What's the difference between oak trees and tight shoes?

One makes acorns and the other makes corns ache.

What do you call a naked grizzly?

Bare.

HA HA HA HA HA
HA HA HA HA HA HA
HA HA HA HA HA HA HA HA

Knock-knock!

Who's there?

Thumping.

Thumping who?

Thumping green is oozing out of your nose.

FOUL FACT

Tigers can have hairballs as big as a football.

What happened when the glassblower inhaled?

He ended up with a pane in his stomach.

Why did the toilet paper roll down the hill?

To get to the bottom.

Mooning is lunacy.

MOM: You should put newspaper in the bathroom for the puppy to use.

KID: Don't be silly! Puppies can't read.

What do you get when you cross peanut-butter candies with mouse droppings?

Meeses Pieces.

Horrible Homework Helper

Don't want the teacher to see that you didn't finish your homework? Crumple it up and use one of these un-*ewww*-usual excuses when you turn it in:

1. "Mom wiped the baby's nose with it.
2. "The dog peed on it."
3. "The cat coughed up a hairball on it."
4. "Dad lined the birdcage with it."
5. "I ran out of TP and grabbed the closest paper."

Knock-knock!

Whos' there?

Wendy.

Wendy who?

Wendy sneeze comes, better duck!

What do you get when you divide a bovine's circumference by its diameter?

Cow pi.

How are horseflies like laxatives?

> **They irritate the poop out of you.**

- -

FOUL FACT

> The male Darwin's frog slurps up his own tadpoles and keeps them in his vocal sac. After about two months, he pukes up fully-formed frogs.

- -

DAD: I thought I told you to eat your mushed peas.

KID: I did.

DAD: Then what's that on your plate?

KID: Mushed pea vomit.

WOOPS

- -

What did the floor say to the chest?

> **"I can see your drawers!"**

- -

HA HA HA HA HA HA HA HA HA HA HA HA HA HA HA

BARF BURGERS

What's the difference between a slug and a peanut-butter cracker?

Slugs don't stick to the roof of your mouth.

- -

KID: Mom, are worms good to eat?

MOM: Why do you ask?

KID: There was one in your salad.

- -

Why do zombies avoid crematoriums?

Everyone's overcooked.

- - - - - - - - - - - - - -

STUDENT: Yuck! There's a fly in my soup!

LUNCH LADY: Don't worry. The spider on your roll will eat it.

- -

FOUL FACT

Ancient Romans ate flamingo tongues.

What's gross?

Finding a hair in your food.

What's grosser than gross?

It's a nose hair.

- -

When do dragons like knights?

When they're roasted and covered in ketchup.

- -

What's the difference between a worm and a chocolate-chip cookie?

A worm doesn't fall apart when you dunk it in milk.

- -

GRODYNITION

Cannibal: a person who goes to a restaurant and orders a waiter.

- -

What did the vulture say before dinner?

Let us prey.

- -

What do dogfish eat?

Guppy chow.

- -

Why do vultures go to lousy restaurants?

Because the food's always rotten.

Knock-knock!

Who's there?

Pasta.

Pasta who?

Pasta brains, I'm hungry.

- -

What does T-rex call bicyclists?

Meals on wheels.

- -

Why wouldn't the kid who'd eat anything refuse to eat 288 roaches?

It was too gross.

- -

What does an ogre call a crowded hot tub?

Soup.

- -

FOUL FACT

Castoreum, an ingredient that adds flavor to raspberry ice cream, comes from a gland located in the butt end of beavers.

- -

Which Spanish city has the worst food?

Barf-a-lona.

- -

Why do zombies prefer smart kids?

They have the biggest br-ai-ai-ains!

- -

HA HA HA HA HA HA HA HA HA HA

What do cannibals eat for breakfast?

Buttered host.

- -

What's the difference between boiled cabbage and boogers?

Kids won't eat boiled cabbage.

- -

Why didn't Batman catch any fish?

Robin ate all the worms.

- -

Knock-knock!

Who's there?

Eton.

Eton who?

Eton out of the garbage.

- - - - - - - - - - - - - - - - - - - -

Should zombies eat brains on an empty stomach?

No. They should eat them on a plate.

- - - - - - - - - - - - - - - - - - - -

FOUL FACT

In Japan, you can buy tuna eyeballs in most grocery stores. Once you boil them, they're said to taste like squid. Ready to try some? We didn't think so.

17

HA HA HA HA HA

Why did the vulture cross the road?

He wanted squash for lunch.

How do you stop a rooster from crowing on Sunday?

Cook him on Saturday.

SNOBBY DINER: This meal isn't fit for a pig!
WAITER: I'll bring back one that is.

Which restaurant charges $10 a head?

The Cannibal Café.

Why did the monster buffet run out of food?

The first one there was a goblin.

FOUL FACT

"Parson's Nose" is a popular treat in Asia. What is it? Grilled chicken butt.

DINER: Waiter! What's this roach doing on my ice cream?

WAITER: Snowboarding.

Why do maggots eat puke?

It's a dirty job, but someone's got to do it.

Why was the cannibal screaming mad?

Because he was fed up with people.

Why does Dracula drink blood?

Root beer makes him burp.

GRODYNITION

Butter: A ram's favorite bread spread.

What time is it when the dog eats the stew Dad made?

Time to get a new dog.

Why do cannibals like to visit nursing homes?

The food is aged to perfection.

What do you do if your burger is crawling with maggots?

Catch it before it gets away.

Cannibal Kid: I don't like my teacher.
Cannibal Dad: Put a little ketchup on her.

HA HA HA HA HA HA

FOUL FACT

An amino acid called L-cysteine helps bread stay fresh. Sound tasty? Think again. Most of it comes from hair swept up from floors in barbershops and hair salons.

What did the frog say to the toad?

Time's fun when you're having flies.

CANNIBAL: Waiter, do you serve senior citizens?
WAITER: Only if we're out of everything else.

What's the best breakfast at The Cemetery Café?

Booscuits and gravey.

Why did the cannibal chase the track star?

He had a craving for fast food.

What's green and gooey on the inside and brown and crunchy on the outside?

A toasted sneeze sandwich.

FOUL FACT

The daddy longlegs spider flosses. How? By pulling its legs through its jaws.

EWWW

HA HA HA HA

Do ghouls eat chicken with their fingers?

No. They eat fingers separately.

What did the toad order with his burger?

A croak-a-cola and flies.

GRODYNITION

Vegetarian: a huge missed steak.

Why do zombies prefer brains to spaghetti?

Brains don't slide off the fork.

Why can't cannibal kids have friends for breakfast?

They are only served for lunch.

FOUL FACT

Male butterflies often drink from puddles. They need the minerals found in them. Among their favorite puddles? Those with urine in them.

Worst School Menu Ever

Pee Soup

Potatoes Au Rotten

Spotted Liver Loaf

Tossed Cookies

CANNIBAL: What did you bring to the party?

HANNIBAL: A kid and a potfer.

CANNIBAL: What's the potfer?

HANNIBAL: To cook the kid, of course.

What's so bad about rabbit pie?

It has hares in it.

Which dish do ghouls order in Chinese restaurants?

Peking yuck.

What do cannibals order at Chinese restaurants?

General Toes.

GRODYNITION

Cocktail: a drink made from a rooster's rear end.

Knock-knock!

Who's there?

Dishes.

Dishes who?

Dishes how I talk with a mouth full of worms.

When is it okay to eat fireflies?

When you just want a light snack.

TWIST THIS

She puked poured cod curd by the sea shore.

- -

SHOPPER: I can't find a turkey big enough to feed my family. Do these get any bigger?
CLERK: No, ma'am. They're dead.

- -

FOUL FACT

Humans aren't at the top of the food chain. Tigers, crocodiles, and boa constrictors are. We're in the middle . . . with the pigs and the anchovies.

- -

What's a vampire's idea of fast food?

Someone with high blood pressure.

SNOT SO FAST!

What green fiend hides in noses?

The boogeyman.

- -

Knock-knock!

Who's not there?

Hippo's not.

HA

Why don't ogres eat boogers?

> **They don't want to spoil their dinner.**

What happened when the teacher sneezed without a tissue?

> **She took matters into her own hands.**

Knock-knock!

> **Who's there?**

Topic.

> **Topic who?**

Topic your nose is gross.

What do you get when a giant sneezes?

> **Out of the way!**

FOUL FACT

> The German word for mucus is *nasenschleim* (nose slime).

Why won't snowmen eat carrot cake?

> **They think it might have boogers in it.**

GIRL: Red hair runs in my family. What runs in yours?

BOY: Noses.

HA HA HA HA HA HA HA HA

GROSSEST BOOK NEVER PUBLISHED: *Green Spots On the Wall* by Picken and Flicken

---

What did the mama pig say to the piglet?

Don't pork your nose.

What's green and slowly drips from trees?

Sloth snot.

FOUL FACT

Some parents suck the snot out of a baby's nose when it can't breathe.

Why didn't the nose make the soccer team?

It didn't get picked.

You can pick your nose and pick your friends, but you can't wipe your friends on the sofa.

Worst Valentine Ever

If you were a booger, I'd pick you!

What's green, sticky, and bounces?

A booger on a pogo stick.

HA HA

WOOPS

Why didn't the viper vipe 'er nose?

Because the adder 'ad 'er handkerchief.

MOM: Why did you put a frog in your sister's bed?

SON: I couldn't collect enough boogers.

Knock-knock!

Who's there?

Swatter.

Swatter who?

Swatter you gonna do with that booger on your finger?

When is a winter storm like a kid with a cold?

When it blows, it snows (its nose).

What do nosepickers like to eat at a cookout?

Hamboogers.

FOUL FACT

Love fast food? A 2015 study showed that 51% of restaurant workers show up when they're sick. That means their germs infect everything you eat.

HA HA HA HA HA
HA HA HA HA HA

Who are the grossest musicians?
    **Banjo players. They're
    always pickin'.**

- - - - - - - - - - - - - - - - - - - -

Why did the little robot take his
nose apart?
    To see what made it run.

- -

**Lulu's so lazy she sticks her nose out the car
window so the wind will blow it for her.**

- -

Why did the nose leave the concert?
    It had to run.

- -

Why did the ghost blow its nose?
    It was full of boo-gers.

- -

What's the difference between a booger and your
butt?
    **Your butt goes ON your chair, a booger goes
    UNDER your chair.**

- -

SIGN SEEN AT A PLASTIC SURGEON'S OFFICE
    Hello! Can we pick your nose?

- -

Why did the nose stop going to school?
    It was tired of getting picked on.

HA HA HA HA

Knock-knock!

    Who's there?

Saul.

    Saul who?

Saul that snot doing on your sleeve?

What do boogers and grapes have in common?

    They both get picked and eaten.

    **If cows laughed, would milk
come out of their noses?**

Why doesn't King Kong pick his nose?

    He doesn't want to eat a five-pound booger.

What do you call someone who never
uses a tissue?

    Greensleeves.

FOUL FACT

    You swallow snot about twice a
minute, even when asleep.

What song do you sing when
the birthday kid is sick?

    Happy Birthday flu you!

STINK BOMBS

What kind of teacher always eats beans for lunch?

A substi-toot.

Grandpa: I just let out a silent fart. What should I do?

Grandma: Replace your hearing aid.

What shoots stuffing across the room?

A farting turkey!

Why do skeletons burp?

They don't have the guts to fart.

GRODYNITION

Eureka: What you say to someone who's been sprayed by a skunk.

How is a ninja like a fart?

They're both silent and deadly.

HA HA HA HA HA HA

Smelly Faves

Movie: *Oh Brother, Where Fart Thou?*

Songs: "Don't Go Breaking My Fart"
and "Go Smell It on the Mountain"

Rock band: Stink Floyd

Who was Egypt's smelliest pharaoh?

King Toot.

What did the boss tell the skunk on its first day at work?

To stink outside the box.

BOY: I have the laziest dog in the world.

GIRL: How do you know?

BOY: I had to water the garden and he didn't lift a leg to help me.

HA

HA HA HA HA HA
HA HA HA HA HA HA HA HA

WIFE: You should be a weatherman.

HUSBAND: Why is that?

WIFE: Because you're such an expert on wind.

FOUL FACT

Marcus Aurelias was only 14 when he became emperor of Rome in 218 CE. His favorite dinner prank? Putting the ancient version of a whoopee cushion on the chairs of those he outranked.

What big green monster reeks?

Stank-enstein's monster.

When's the best time to change a baby's diaper?

In the wee-wee hours of the morning.

What do you get when you cross a fart with a boomerang?

A smell that keeps coming back.

Words skunks live by: Eat, stink, and be merry.

Where do the dirtiest kids go for an education?

Smell-ementary schools.

What do skunks eat with burgers?

Stench fries.

Knock-knock!

Who's there?

Sonya.

Sonya who?

Sonya shoe! I can smell it from here.

WOOPS

How many farts does it take to fill a gym?

Quite a phew.

What do you call a smelly chicken?

A foul fowl.

How bad does a rotten mummy smell?

It Sphinx.

Which football tournament do zombies like best?

The Rotten Bowl.

Five Ways to Fart

1. Loud and proud
2. Silent but violent
3. Ease and squeeze
4. Toot and scoot
5. Hide and squeak

Sis: You must be built upside down.

Bro: Why do you say that?

Sis: Because your nose runs and your feet smell.

Why do delis smell bad?

Someone's always cutting the cheese.

What's black, white, green, and smelly?

Two skunks fighting over a pickle.

Knock-knock!

Who's there?

Gas.

Gas who?

Gas who ate beans for dinner?

FOUL FACT

The two-striped walking stick insect has a stink-a-riffic method of scaring away threats. It shoots disgusting gunk out of a gland behind its head. The stuff smells so bad it leaves everything in its wake gasping for breath.

What's the best way to talk to someone with bad breath?

From across the room.

HA HA HA HA HA HA HA HA

CHESTER: Is your sister spoiled?

JESTER: No. That's just her cheap perfume.

What's the smelliest fish?

The stink-ray.

Why did one eye accuse the other eye of farting?

Something smelled between them.

Knock-knock!

Who's there?

Claws.

Claws who?

Claws the door! There's a skunk out here.

How do mummies clean their ears?

With rotten swabs.

Did you hear about the dog that loved to eat garlic?

His bark was worse than his bite.

DAD: How dare you fart in front of your mother?

SON: Sorry. I didn't know it was Mom's turn.

Where do Unidentified Farting Objects come from?

Uranus.

What's a skunk's favorite sandwich?

Peanut butter and smelly.

Which search engine really stinks?

Poogle.

Which fairy leaves something smelly under your pillow?

The toot fairy.

HA HA

How can you tell when a fly farts?

It flies faster for a few seconds.

Worse Verse

A tutor who tutored the flute
had two fluters he tutored to toot.
But when both fluters tooted,
the air was polluted,
and the tutor ran out of the door.

Why was the cannibal gassy?

He ate too many human beans.

When does kindness stink?

When you pick up a hitchhiker who hasn't showered in two weeks.

FOUL FACT

The Anthropological Research Facility (ARF) in Tennessee studies how bodies decompose. The smell of rotting bodies led locals to nickname the place "BARF."

Farting on an elevator is wrong on every level.

Why can't Dracula get a date?

He has bat breath.

Why did the skunk get kicked out of the comedy club?

His jokes all stank.

This book smells: *Bubbles in the Bath* by Iva Windybottom

How do you keep a trash collector from smelling?

Hold his nose.

What did the farmer say to the sheep that stepped in a cow pie?

Ewe stink!

WATCH OUT!

The eastern spotted skunk does a handstand before it sprays.

What's invisible and smells like carrots?

Rabbit farts.

What do you get when you cross a skunk with perfume?

Whatever it is, don't smell it!

What's yellow and smells of brains?

Zombie puke.

Why do giraffes need such long necks?

Because their feet stink.

FOUL FACT

Stinky feet are caused by bacteria. The bacteria gobble up the sweat on feet and poop out smelly waste.

What's worse than a fart?

A fart with a lump in it.

HA HA

MA: We can't keep goats in the house. Think of the smell!

PA: Don't worry. The goats will get used to it.

World's Worst Read: *Something Smells* by I. Ben Pharting

Which fish has no sense of smell?

A dead one.

GRODYNITION

Extinct: a dead skunk.

LITTLE SIS: If frozen tea is iced tea, what's frozen ink?

BIG BRO: Iced ink.

LITTLE SIS: Then you should take a bath.

World's Stinkiest Names

Wendy Rump

Stan K. Pitts

Ivan Oder

Anita Bathe

Jim Sox

Chuck Upson

Knock-knock!

Who's there?

Mop.

Mop who?

What a stinky thing to say!

FOUL FACT

Motto of the town of Gas, Kansas: "Don't pass Gas! Stop and enjoy it."

Why did the man eat ten cans of baked beans?

He wanted to go wind-surfing.

DR. PUKE

What did the vampire doctor say?

Necks, please!

PATIENT: Doctor! Doctor! I've got wind! Can you help?

DOCTOR: Sure. Here's a kite.

How can you tell the difference between an oral and a rectal thermometer?

The taste.

How do you know your breath stinks?

Your dentist will only treat you over the phone.

Why did the terrible teacher visit the eye doctor?

She'd just lost another pupil.

FOUL FACT

In the 1700s, a Philadelphia doctor tried to find out how yellow fever was spread. He fed his patients' vomit to birds, cats, and dogs to see if the animals would get sick. They didn't. Next, he tried to get people to volunteer. They didn't, so he drank the vomit himself.

Why did the toilet go to the doctor?

It was feeling flushed.

PATIENT: Doctor, doctor! Is eating red meat bad for you?

DOCTOR: Not as bad as eating green meat.

GRODYNITION

Tissue: cold storage

HA HA

HA HA HA HA HA

CURIOUS KID: Which one of those trees is a weeping willow?
NATURE GUIDE: The one that needs a root canal.

What happened when the toddler ate a whole box of animal crackers?

He tossed his cookies.

PATIENT: Doctor, doctor! I'm at death's door!
DOCTOR: Don't worry. I'll pull you through.

What's chunky, smelly, and goes up and down?

A puddle of puke in an elevator.

Why did Jackie Chan visit the doctor?

He had Kung Flu.

Knock-knock!

Who's there?

Avocado.

Avocado who?

Avocado cold so I can't come to school.

What's the difference between a banana and an infected wound?

One bruises; the other oozes.

What was Doctor Jekyll's favorite game?

Hyde and seek.

FOUL FACT

Dollar bills are oozing with bacteria.
The most common?
The bacteria that
causes acne.

Knock-knock!

Who's there?

Ivan.

Ivan who?

Ivan infectious disease.

Go away! Nobody's home.

What animal always pukes after lunch?

The yak.

PATIENT: Nurse! I need to see the doctor. I've only got fifty-nine seconds to live.

NURSE: Don't worry. He'll be with you in a just a minute.

What do you get when you eat pizza out of the garbage?

Pizza-rhea.

PATIENT: Does an apple a day really keep the doctor away?

NURSE: Only if you aim well enough.

Knock, knock!

Who's there?

Stan.

Stan who?

Stan back, I'm about to hurl.

PATIENT: Doctor, doctor! Can you do anything else for my pimples?

DOCTOR: No. That zit.

CHARLES: Doctor, doctor! I fell off the exam table.

DOCTOR: Up, Chuck!

PATIENT: Doctor, doctor! Do you have a cure for nail biting?

DOCTOR: Sure! Cut off your fingers.

PATIENT: I can't get rid of this constipation.

DOCTOR: Try sitting on the toilet and hitting yourself on the head.

PATIENT: Why would I do that?

DOCTOR: Works for ketchup.

HA HA HA HA HA HA HA HA

HA HA HA HA HA

What do you get if you eat a whole cake?

A happy barf-day!

FOUL FACT

Don't pick that scab! Scabs are nature's bandaids. They keep germs out of a wound while it heals.

KID: Mom, I'm too sick to go to school.

MOM: It's snot for you to decide.

What do you call ghost vomit?

Spook puke.

PATIENT: Doctor, doctor! How do I cure this splitting headache?

DOCTOR: Take the ax out of your head.

NEARSIGHTED SUE: Did you hear about the optometrist who fell into his lens grinder?

FARSIGHTED SAL: Yes! He made a spectacle of himself.

What made the lion's belly ache?

Someone he ate.

Did you hear about the giant who threw up?

Of course. It was all over town.

What do you get when you cross tacos with a bellyache?

I don't know, but you're standing in it.

GRODYNITION

Acupuncture: a jab well done.

Why do mommy birds puke in baby birds' mouths every morning?

So they'll have a hot meal.

What does a dog say when it's eaten something rotten?

Barf! Barf!

What happened when the judge got poison ivy?

She made rash decisions.

Why didn't the girl tell the doctor she'd swallowed glue?

Her lips were sealed.

HA HA HA HA HA HA HA HA
HA HA HA HA HA HA HA HA

FOUL FACT

Space sickness makes astronauts barf. The good news: they have super-strong barf bags. The bad news: they have to keep them in the ship with them until they return to Earth.

PATIENT: Doctor, doctor! Can I catch dandruff?
DOCTOR: Sure. Just shake your head over a paper bag.

What do you call a knight with stomach flu?
Sir Pukes-a-lot.

PATIENT: Doctor, doctor! I need something for my liver!
DOCTOR: Try onions.

SIS: Your breath reminds me of being in a boat at sea.
BRO: How so?
SIS: It makes me want to hurl.

What's a surefire way to get a ride to the hospital?
Step in front of an ambulance.

Which noodles always have a cold?

Mac and sneeze.

- -

PATIENT: Doctor, doctor! Why did you drop that newborn baby?
DOCTOR: Because it's a ghoul.

- -

Which animals make the worst doctors?

Ducks. They're all quacks.

- -

Why did the Big Bad Wolf visit the doctor?

He had hood-in-mouth disease.

- -

How do you know your surgeon is funny?

He leaves you in stitches.

- -

Knock-knock!

Who's there?

Claire.

Claire who?

Claire the way! I'm gonna spew.

- - - - - - - - - - - - - - -

HA HA HA

Worse Verse

There was a young girl named Rose
who had a large wart on her nose.
She had it removed,
her looks were improved,
but her glasses slid down to her toes.

Which airline uses the most barf-bags?
Spew-nited.

PATIENT: Doctor, doctor! I hate this toenail fungus.
DOCTOR: Don't worry. It'll grow on you.

How long should doctors practice medicine?
Until they get it right.

PATIENT: Doctor, doctor! I just swallowed a bone.
DOCTOR: Are you choking?
PATIENT: No. I'm serious.

What's brown and sits on a piano bench?

Beethoven's last movement.

TOOTHBRUSH: I hate my job!
TOILET PAPER: Want to trade?

FOUL FACT

America's pet dogs produce 10.6 million tons of poop every year.

What do you call a farmer who steps in a cow pie?

An in-cow-poop.

Why did the soldier change the baby's diaper?

Because doody called.

Which musical instrument takes bathroom breaks?

The pee-ano.

What would you find in the pot after eating a giant tortoise?

Giant turdles.

HA HA HA HA HA HA HA HA HA HA HA HA HA

FOUL FACT

In 1669, a German alchemist tried to turn pee into gold. First he peed into a bathtub. Next he boiled the pee into a paste. Did it turn into gold? Nope. But when he heated the stinky stuff again, it did go boom and burst into flame. How foul (and fun) is that?

You know what they say about a bird in the hand . . . it poops in your palm.

Knock-knock!

Who's there?

European.

European who?

European all over the place. Aim for the toilet!

What happens after eating four cans of alphabet soup?

A massive vowel movement.

PIGEON 1: What do you want to do today?

PIGEON 2: Let's go over to the car lot and put a deposit on a new car.

FOUL FACT

Some eco-minded companies now sell reusable toilet wipes. Sound gross? Yes. Yes, it does.

What's the smelliest letter in the alphabet?

P.

Why didn't anyone see the movie *Constipation*?

It never came out.

What famous dump happened in Boston Harbor in 1773?

The Boston Tea Potty.

What do polar bears get from sitting on the toilet for too long?

Polaroids!

Which book in a trilogy always stinks?

The turd.

FOUL FACT

Pandas poop 50 times a day.

Why did the toddler sit under a cow?

She wanted a pat on the head.

HA HA HA HA HA HA HA HA HA HA

What happens when you have a bladder infection?

Urine trouble.

HUGH: We just sold our Bengal cat for $1,000.

STU: Wow! We just sold our Great Dane.

HUGH: What did you sell it for?

STU: For pooping on the floor.

If pigs really could fly . . . we'd need bigger umbrellas.

What's the German word for "fart"?

Farfrompoopin.

FOUL FACT

Astronaut Buzz Aldrin peed in his spacesuit on the Moon. It was a lunar first!

Did you hear about the constipated accountant?

He couldn't budget.

How do toilets keep in touch?

Pee-mail.

GRODYNITION

Urine: where you are when you're not out.

HA HA HA HA HA HA HA HA

What do you call tiger poop?

Endangered feces.

What's big and brown and behind a wall?

Humpty's dump.

EWWW

FOUL FACT

Never pee in the Amazon River. Why? Because a tiny sucker fish will swim up the pee stream into your body. Once it gets inside, it launches little hooks to hold its place and feeds off your blood.

What do stockings have in common with people who have diarrhea?

They both get runs down their legs.

BOY: Can I go to the bathroom?

TEACHER: Only if you can sing the alphabet song.

BOY: OK. A-B-C-D-E-F-G-H-I-J-K-L-M-N-O . . . Q-R-S-T-U-V-W-X-Y and Z!

TEACHER: Where's the P?

BOY: Running down my leg.

HA HA HA

GRODYNITION

Scatomancy: Telling the future by looking at turds.

- -

What did one dung beetle ask the other dung beetle?

Is this stool taken?

- -

Knock-knock!

Who's there?

Bea.

Bea who?

Bea sweet and wipe the seat.

- -

Worse Verse

A belch is just a gust of wind,
That cometh from thy heart . . .
But should it take the downward trend,
It turns into a fart.

- -

How do you escape from a locked bathroom stall?

With a doo-key.

- -

HA HA HA HA HA
HA HA HA HA HA HA HA HA
HA HA HA HA HA

HA HA HA HA HA HA HA

Why did the kid bring a dirty diaper to school?

For show and smell.

FOUL FACT

The character Hercule Poirot in the TV adaptation of Agatha Christie's murder mystery books had a very special gait. To "walk like a detective," the actor clenched a coin between his buttocks.

What did the first mate find in the ship's toilet?

The captain's log.

Inside a fire hydrant: H_2O.
Outside a fire hydrant: K-9P.

What do you get when you cross an outhouse with a famous wizard?

A Harry Potty.

How do you keep school boys on their toes?

Raise the urinals.

What do you need when you cross an elephant with a poodle?

A bigger pooper scooper.

HA HA HA HA HA HA HA HA HA HA HA HA HA HA HA HA HA HA HA HA HA HA HA

FOUL FACT

Even Olympic swimmers pee in the pool.

Why couldn't the toilet paper cross the road?

It was stuck in a crack.

What will you never see a plumber do?

Bite his nails.

Knock-knock!

Who's there?

Ahab.

Ahab who?

Ahab to go to the bathroom.

BATHROOM READING: *Go and Go Again* by Di A. Rhea

Scariest movie when you gotta go?

Invasion of the Potty Snatchers.

How do you keep flies out of the kitchen?

Move the chamber pot to the living room.

What do you call it when you step in alien droppings?

A close encounter of the turd kind.

What should you do if you find a python in your toilet?

Wait until it's finished.

Bathroom Nationalities

Hurrying into the stall: *Russian*

In the stall: *European*

On the way out: *Finnish*

KID: I had trouble with diarrhea in class today.

DAD: That's awful. I didn't know you were sick.

KID: I'm not. I just couldn't spell it.

Knock-knock!

Who's there?

Annie One.

Annie One who?

Annie One know where to find some toilet paper?

WENDY RUMP: What do you clean your top teeth with?

MO RAHN: A toothbrush.

WENDY RUMP: And your bottom?

MO RAHN: The same.

WENDY RUMP: Oh, gross! I use toilet paper.

Why did the kid name his puppy Carpenter?

Because he kept doing little jobs all over the house.

FOUL FACT

Want your poo to turn red? Eat a lot of beets!

What nut can you find in the toilet?

A peanut.

HA HA

DEAD FUNNY

How do zombies say good-bye?
"It's been nice gnawing you."

What has four legs and flies?
A dead cow.

Why did the little ghoul stay home from school?
She was feeling rotten.

What are a zombie's least favorite letters?
D-K (decay).

What should a gravedigger never do?
Throw himself into his work.

GROSS QUOTE
"Three may keep a secret, if two are dead."
—Benjamin Franklin

Who do gravediggers invite to their parties?
Anyone they can dig up.

HA HA HA HA HA HA

What was the mummy's favorite kind of music?

Rot and roll.

Why did the veterinarian stop treating toads?

They all croaked.

Knock-knock!

Who's there?

Just chicken.

Just chicken who?

Just chicken to see if you're alive.

Which brothers started the first cemetery?

Doug and Phil Graves.

What did the skeleton order at the soda fountain?

Two root beers and a mop.

What's a zombie's favorite vegetable?

Corn on the corpse.

GRODYNITION

Burial plot: the last thing you'll ever need.

LOL

Why was the zookeeper who fed the otters fired?

He fed them to the sharks.

How are undertakers like movie stars?

People are dying to meet them.

FOUL FACT

Within three days after death, the enzymes that once digested your lunch begin to digest you!

What sport do mummies play?

Casketball.

HA HA

Why do undertakers prefer cremation?

Because they urn more.

Why was the skeleton always sad?

A dog ran away with its funny bone.

What is Bach doing in his grave?

Decomposing.

When's the worst time to bury someone?

When they're still breathing.

Why couldn't the cannibal sell his house?

He was asking for an arm and a leg.

Why was the corpse upset?
    He made a grave error.

Why did the ghost ride an elevator?
    To lift his spirits.

Where do zombies buy food?
    At the gore-cery store.

Knock-knock!
    Who's there?
Waddle.
    Waddle who?
Waddle I do with this corpse
on the porch?

How did the zombies win
the football game?
    **They kicked a field
    ghoul.**

If a man was born in Mexico, grew up in America,
and died in France, what is he?
    Dead.

**HA HA HA HA HA HA HA HA
HA HA HA HA HA HA**

HA HA HA HA HA HA HA HA HA HA HA HA HA

Never Say Die

Old printers never die. They're just not the type.

Old milk maids never die. They just lose their whey.

Old cashiers never die. They just check out.

Old janitors never die. They just kick the bucket.

Old hackers never die. They just go to bits.

LITTLE ZOMBIE: Mom, can I have my new best friend over for dinner?

MOMMY ZOMBIE: Not until we finish eating your old one.

Why can't a man marry his widow's sister?

Because he's dead.

Why did the corpse call the doctor?

He had worms.

FOUL FACT

"Mummy brown" was once a popular paint color for artists. Unfortunately, the company that made it ran out of the main ingredient: actual ground up Egyptian mummies.

Why did the zombie go to the fanciest restaurant in town?

He wanted a three-corpse meal.

Here Lies Grandma: She always said her feet were killing her, but no one believed her.

Why can't the Zombies outrun the Vampires?

Every race ends in a dead heat.

FOUL FACT

Think zombies are bad? Sea squirts attach themselves to rocks and then . . . eat their own brai-ai-ai-ains!

Deadly Businesses

Zombie Hair Salon: *Curl Up and Die*

Vampire Shop: *Fangs for Coming In*

Cannibal Café: *We Serve You First!*

Why don't ghouls go to zombie parties?

They don't want to lose face.

Which whales don't swim?

Dead ones.

Why did the cannibal call the morgue?

He wanted to know if they delivered.

Tongueless Twisters
(for zombies and skeletons)

Ea-er iper icke uh eck of ickle eppers.

E elle ee ells aiee uh ee ore.

Uzzy uzzy uz uh air

Uzzy uzzy ah oh air

Uzzy uzzy uzz'n uzzy, uz ee?

What killed the Italian chef?

He pasta way.

What was written on the tomb of the person who invented AutoCorrect?

Wrest in piece.

What should you always be grateful for on Thanksgiving?

That you're not a turkey.

FOUL FACT

When renters stopped paying for a 10-by-10-foot storage unit, management decided to auction off the contents. What did they find? Grandma! The mummified remains of the renter's grandmother were found inside a blue casket. She'd been there for 17 years.

What do you call a dead magician?

An abracadaver.

What do a toilet and a coffin have in common?

When you gotta go, you gotta go.

What happened to the wordy writer?

She was sentenced to death.

What do gravediggers put in their coffee?

Burial grounds.

What is the worst way for a balloon to relax?

Acupuncture.

HA HA HA HA HA HA HA HA HA HA

Why did the undertaker tie his clients' shoelaces together?

He wanted to add humor to the zombie apocalypse.

Where did the skeleton keep his pet parrot?

In a rib cage.

FOUL FACT

No bull: A Brazilian man was killed by a cow that fell through the roof of his house. Seems his house backed up to a hillside. The 3,000 pound cow wandered onto the roof and crashed through, landing on the man's bed while he slept. Neither his wife (who was sleeping beside him) nor the cow were injured.

What kind of roads lead into graveyards?

Dead ends.

What is the cannibal's favorite game?

Swallow the leader.

Deadliest Memoir: *A Mortician's Tale* by I. M. Balm

What killed The Mummy?

Mold age.

SLIME AFTER SLIME

How do you make a snail drink?
Put it in a blender.

- -

What is slimy and grants wishes?
The Wizard of Ooze.

- -

What does the podiatrist put on his toast?
Toe jam.

- -

Why did the kid toss a slug out the window?
He wanted to see slime fly.

- -

What is tall, green, gooey, and has bolts in its neck?
Franken-slime's monster.

- -

MOM: You look pretty dirty.
DAUGHTER: Thanks! I look even prettier when I'm clean.

- -

What's green, sticky, and smells like eucalyptus?
Koala vomit.

- -

HA HA HA HA HA HA HA HA
HA HA HA HA HA HA HA HA

FOUL FACT

Some face creams include snail slime. Why?
Because it smooths wrinkles.

- - - - - - - - - - - - - - -

What is the Blob's
favorite drink?
Slime-ade.

- -

How do you find the grossest
slime jokes?
You goo-gle them.

- -

Do slugs get arrested for jaywalking?
No. It's a victimless slime.

- -

How do slugs send messages?
They use snail mail.

- -

FOUL FACT

Blennophobia is the fear of slime.

- -

What did The Blob write on his postcard to his
mom?
Wish goo were here!

- -

How do slugs vacation?
On an ooze ship.

HA HA HA HA HA

Worse Verse

My fangs drip slime, my nose drips snot,
I slurp and belch and fart a lot.
My ears ooze wax. My zits drip pus.
What am I? Disgusting!

How do fairytales for slugs begin?

Once upon a slime . . .

Knock-knock!

Who's there?

Ooze.

Ooze who?

Ooze in charge around here?

GRODYNITION

Jam: A jellyfish that just got stepped on.

BABY RATTLER: Mom, are we venomous?

MOMMY RATTLER: Yes. Why do you ask?

BABY RATTLER: I just bit my tongue.

Why didn't The Blob like his little sister?

She was a goody two-ooze.

What's a snail's favorite dessert?
Key Slime Pie.

What do you get when you cross a whale with The Blob?
Moby Ick.

Why can't snails and slugs go to school together?
They live in different slime zones.

What's the best advice to give a worm?
Sleep late.

FOUL FACT

The 1958 movie *The Blob* was based on something that really happened. A mysterious object fell from the sky in Philadelphia. Police who arrived on the scene found a huge mound of purple slime. It seemed to be oozing up a telephone pole as if alive.

What do you call two slugs on a rug?
A pair of slippers.

Which kind of barbeque does The Blob like best?
Slime Ribs.

HA HA HA HA HA

Knock-knock!
>**Who's there?**

Ooze.
>**Ooze who?**

Ooze going to change the baby's diaper?

Who's the oiliest politician of all?
>**The Slime Minister of Grease.**

What flavor popsicles do ghouls like best?
>**Lemon-slime.**

Why is everyone scared of the Blobfather?
>**He heads up the biggest slime family.**

FOUL FACT
>Navy Seals sometimes wear pantyhose. Why?
>To keep leeches off their legs.

Why did the police put yellow tape around
the garden?
>**It was a slime scene.**

What's The Blob's favorite kind of music?
>**Rhythm and Ooze.**

**Never judge a snail until you
walk a mile in its ooze.**

What do you call monster spit?
  Ghoul drool.

What's The Blob's favorite game show?
  Goo Wants to Be a Millionaire.

Why was the banana slug arrested for robbery?
  He was the slime suspect.

SLIMIEST BOOK NEVER WRITTEN: *An Oyster's
Life* by Ima Shellfish

What's the difference between a school lunch and
a pile of slugs?
  School lunches come on a plate.

FOUL FACT
  Hagfish got the nickname "slime eel" because
  they look like eels and they can ooze enough
  slime to fill a bucket in just a few minutes.

Why did the janitor ask the lunch lady to clean up
the barf in the cafeteria?
  They were partners in grime.

What Golden Rule do little slugs learn?
>Goo unto others
>as they goo
>unto you.

YIKES!

- - - - - - - - - - - -

GRODYNITION
>**Slug:** A snail
>with a housing
>problem.

GASPS FROM THE PAST

Which president was hit by a train?
>**George Squashington.**

- -

Which Roman leader always had a cold?
>**Julius Sneezer.**

- -

Why was General Custer buried at West Point?
>**Because he was dead.**

- -

What happened when the butcher backed into the meat grinder?
>**He got a little behind in his work.**

- -

HA HA HA HA HA HA HA HA HA HA

HA HA HA HA HA HA HA HA HA HA HA HA HA HA HA HA HA HA

Why were Grandma's stockings so wrinkly?

She didn't wear stockings.

What do you get if you throw a grenade into Napoleon's kitchen?

Linoleum Blownaparte.

FOUL FACT

For the final 79 days of his life, President Garfield was fed a mix of broth, blood, and whiskey . . . through his anus.

How is a card game like Queen Victoria visiting a bathroom?

Both end with a royal flush.

GRODYNITION

Liberty: Paul Revere's favorite drink.

Who was the biggest jokester in the Revolutionary War?

Laughfayette.

What do you call maggoty meat, rotten eggs, and moldy bread?

Grosseries.

Why did Vladimir Lenin fall into the latrine?

He was Russian.

Why does the ghost of Anne Boleyn keep chasing the ghost of Henry VIII?

She's trying to get ahead.

Why did the grandpa wear eyeglasses on his bottom?

He was fart-sighted.

Grossest Book Never Published: *Rusty Bedsprings* by I.P. Nightly

---

Why didn't people in the Dark Ages have fleas in their hair.

The lice ate them.

FOUL FACT

Elizabeth Bathory, a Hungarian countess, was hungry for blood. How hungry? She earned the name "The Blood Countess" by bathing in the blood of peasant girls. She thought it would keep her young and beautiful.

HA HA HA HA
HA HA HA HA HA HA HA HA

Why did the lion throw up after eating Gandhi?

Because it's hard to keep a good man down.

Which World War II general wore the smelliest boots?

The one with the stinkiest feet.

GROSS QUOTE

"Guests, like fish, begin to smell after a few days."—Benjamin Franklin

---

TOUR GUIDE: What has eyes but can't see, ears but can't hear, and can jump as high as the Washington Monument?

TOURIST: I don't know.

TOUR GUIDE: A dead cat.

TOURIST: But a dead cat can't jump!

TOUR GUIDE: Neither can the Washington Monument.

Why don't mummies like to dance?

They're always dead on their feet.

What's yellow, lumpy, and hurtles past Earth every 75 years?

Halley's Vomit.

What happened when Houdini included his sister in his magic act?

He ended up with two half sisters.

Why is England the soggiest country?

The Queen has reigned there for decades.

FOUL FACT

"You have a turd in your teeth" was a common insult in 17th-century England.

Why were the Salem witch trials so serious?

There was a lot at stake.

Why did George Washington's kids give him Beano® for his birthday?

Because he was the farter of our country.

Why did the venomous viper bite Cleopatra?

Because it was an asp.

How were the Pilgrims like ants?
They lived in colonies.

Why didn't Abraham Lincoln make it to Gettysburg?
He forgot the address.

What did the captain of the *Mayflower* say to the pigs in the ship's hold?
Stop swining! We're almost there!

What was written on the Black Knight's tombstone?
Rust in Peace.

What cologne do dead presidents wear?
Mold Spice.

When did Cleopatra die?
Shortly before her funeral.

HISTORY TEACHER: What was Dorothea Lange known for?
STUDENT: Shooting people and blowing them up.
HISTORY TEACHER: Wrong.
STUDENT: No. It's true! She was a photographer.

HA HA HA HA HA

If two wrongs don't make a right, what do two rights make?

An airplane.

Who was married to Whistler's Mother?

Whistler's Father.

FOUL FACT

In the earliest games of football, players tossed inflated pigs' bladders (hopefully not still filled with pee).

Why were the mammoths kicked out of the swimming pool?

Because they couldn't keep their trunks up.

Why didn't Plato like fried food?

Because it was cooked in Ancient Greece.

What did King George III say about the American Colonies?

"They're revolting."

FOUL FACT

In 2002, the government of Malawi was accused of working with vampires. What were they supposed to be up to? Collecting blood for international aid agencies.

- -

American history is a thing of the past.

- -

Why did the Pilgrims' pants always fall down?
Because their buckles were on their hats.

- -

GROSS QUOTE

"He that dines on stale flesh, especially with the addition of onions, shall be able to afford a stink that no company can tolerate."
—Benjamin Franklin

- -

Why did Florence Nightingale bring a red marker to work?
In case she had to draw blood.

- -

HISTORY TEACHER: Do you know the 16th president of the United States?
STUDENT: No. We were never introduced.

- -

Which Civil War general slept with his dogs?
Robert E. Flea.

- -

FOUL FACT

France's King Louis XVI's neck was too fat for the guillotine. That didn't stop his beheading by French Revolutionaries, but it did increase the bleeding enough to fill a bucket.

What did the explorer say when he saw his first mountain lion?

"I just puma pants."

Which musician was always depressed?

Miles Davis. He was the king of the blues.

Knock-knock!

Who's there?

Manure.

Manure who?

Manure jokes are older than history.

HA

How was the Roman Empire cut in half?

With a pair of Caesars.

FOUL FACT

Before refrigeration, Russians dropped live frogs into milk to keep it from spoiling. How did it work? Their skin is loaded with compounds that kill deadly bacteria.

How long did Sir Isaac Newton live?

All his life.

Was Benjamin Franklin surprised when he discovered electricity?

Yes! It was quite a shock.

How did early Americans keep milk from going sour?

They left it in the cows.

Why did Pavarotti have such a high voice?

It was his falsetto teeth.

FOUL FACT

Count Dracula the vampire is fictional. But he's based on a real Romanian prince. Vlad Dracula lived in the 1400s. To terrify his enemies, he impaled them on stakes.

How do you turn Albert Einstein into a mad scientist?

Stomp on his foot.

STEWARD TO SEASICK PASSENGER: Shall I serve dinner in your cabin?

PASSENGER: No. Just throw it overboard and save me the trouble.

EXTRA GROSS

What has fifty heads but still can't think straight?

A teen with zits.

- -

MOM: Your dad thinks he's an alligator.

KID: What do you think we should do?

MOM: Make him into a handbag and a pair of shoes.

- -

FOUL FACT

The outer layer of your skin is made up of dead skin cells.

- -

Which teacher never farts in public?

A private tooter.

- -

HA HA HA HA HA HA HA HA HA HA

HA HA HA HA HA HA HA HA HA HA

Why did the sports fan spend so much time in the bathroom?

He liked to watch the toilet bowl.

Which monsters are the most stressed out?

Mummies. They're always wound up.

Teacher: Please use the word "gruesome" in a sentence.

Student: My sister stopped shaving her legs and gruesome hair.

When do boys take bubble baths?

**When they eat beans
for dinner.**

FOUL FACT

Reindeer have to pee every six miles.
It's true! They do. In Finland, *poronkusema*—
reindeer urine—has been used as a measure of distance.

What was the trash collector's favorite dance?

The garbage can-can.

LITTLE GHOUL: Mommy do I have Daddy's eyes?

MOMMY GHOUL: Yes, dear. Now eat them before they get cold.

What's the best use of cowhide?

Keeping a cow's guts inside.

When is it better to give than to receive?

When you're having a snowball fight.

GHOUL: I want to hold your hand.

GHOULFRIEND: Only if you promise to give it back.

How do you keep a kid from biting his nails?

Cut off his fingers.

KID: What are you going to do with that pile of manure?

GARDENER: I'm going to put it on my strawberries.

KID: Yuck! I put whipped cream on mine.

HA HA HA HA HA
HA HA HA HA HA
HA HA HA HA HA

Vile Vocabulary

clatterfart: a gossip
fanny-blower: a 19th century slang for fan
fartlek: Swedish for interval training
pakapoo: Australian word for a lottery

Why did the three little warthogs run away from home?

Their father was a dreadful boar.

What happens when you drop a piano down a mine shaft?

You get a flat miner (minor).

How are crosswalks like music?

If you don't C-sharp you will B-flat.

What should you do if a zombie rolls his eyes at you?

Roll them back.

What is green, gooey, and hidden under your bed?

The boogie man.

What do you get if you cross a pig with a young goat?

A dirty kid.

I have an open mouth filled with flesh and blood, skin and bone, and my tongue hangs out. What am I?

A shoe.

Insultingly Gross: That kid moves so slow all he can outrun are his farts.

What do you get for making the world's best fried chicken?

The Nobel Grease Prize.

Which drawers have no handles?

Underwear.

What do you get when you put a canary in a blender?

Shredded tweet.

What do you call a bigfoot prince?

The hair apparent.

HA   HA   HA   HA

GRODYNITION

Explain: a plane after it crashes.

How do you make tear gas?

Mix onions with beans.

Why was the turkey kicked out of the
Thanksgiving feast?

For using fowl language.

FOUL FACT

In 2018, doctors in China removed a tapeworm
from a man's brain. It was nearly four inches
long and still alive.

What was the earth worm's best school subject?

English de-composition.

Why did the witch dye her hair green?

She wanted it to match her teeth.

Why doesn't Frankenstein like joke books?

They make him laugh his head off.

LOL

Itchiest Beach Read: *Sitting on the Shore* by Sandy Bottom

GRODYNITION

Hogwash: a pig's underwear hanging on a clothesline.

What do you get when you cross a monkey with a stick of dynamite?

A ba-boom!

FOUL FACT

Some people can hear their own eyeballs moving. It's caused by a tiny hole in a bone covering part of the inner ear.

Why did the slow driver scrub the toilets in the gas station?

The sign outside said, "Clean restrooms."

How do you make a slow horse fast?

Refuse to feed him.

HA HA HA HA HA HA HA HA

HA HA HA HA HA HA HA HA HA HA

What's black and white and red all over?

An exploding penguin.

Why did the janitor lose his job?

He was always talking trash.

GRODYNITION

Hangnail: a coat hook.

Why did the hyena have five legs?

It stole the lion's leftovers.

What do you give a mouse with bad breath?

Mousewash.

Why was the boy's mom so upset when he came home with a broken nose?

It wasn't his.

How do you win a fight with an octopus?

Disarm it.

What's a pig's favorite music?

Hip-slop.

Which ogre is always angry?

The one with the monster wedgie.

Which mad scientist is a fan of recycling?

Dr. Frankenstein.

FOUL FACT

In 2004, airport security at Boston's Logan airport found a seal's head in a biology professor's suitcase. He was allowed to board the plane. The severed head was not.

When do teens break up?

When zit's all over.

GARBAGE COLLECTOR: Should we shoo the flies?

COLLECTOR 2: No. They can go barefoot.

What's the difference between a short witch and a fleeing buck?

One's a stunted hag and the other is a hunted stag.

Best Bathtime Reading: *Ten Years in the Tub* by Rink Lee Prune

----

HA HA HA HA HA HA HA HA

HA HA HA HA HA
HA HA HA HA HA HA HA HA
HA HA HA HA HA

What did the zombie write on his ex-girlfriend's card?

I'll always dismember you.

How does a roll of toilet paper feel after a long day at work?

Pooped.

Why did the skeleton have a hard time learning to read?

It didn't have bowels in its vocabulary.

Why were the kids in computer class scratching their heads?

They had inter-nits.

What's the worst kind of snow ice cream?

The yellow kind.

FOUL FACT

A *teratoma* is a kind of tumor that grows inside the human body. They can contain hair and teeth.

TAXI DRIVER: Do you want a lift?

FRENCH HITCHHIKER: Oui! Oui!

TAXI DRIVER: Not in my car you don't.

- -

Scariest Monster T-shirt: I 8 NY

- -

Where do all stories about food finish?

    THE END.

- -

ABOUT THE AUTHOR

Kim T. Griswell has worked for Highlights for Children, The Mailbox Book Company, Boyds Mills Press, and Portable Press, and published short stories, articles, columns, blog posts, and books for educational publishers. Her picture books include *Rufus Goes to School*, *Rufus Goes to Sea*, and *Rufus Blasts Off!* (all Sterling; the first two were Oregon Book Awards finalists). In addition, Kim has taught writing workshops, visited schools, and has done readings of her work across the country. She and her husband live in Ashland, OR.

Find out more about Kim at kimgriswell.com.